THE SCIENCE OF...

FORENSIC INVESTIGATION

by
BRIAN INNES
Consultant
ALLISON JONES

CONTENTS

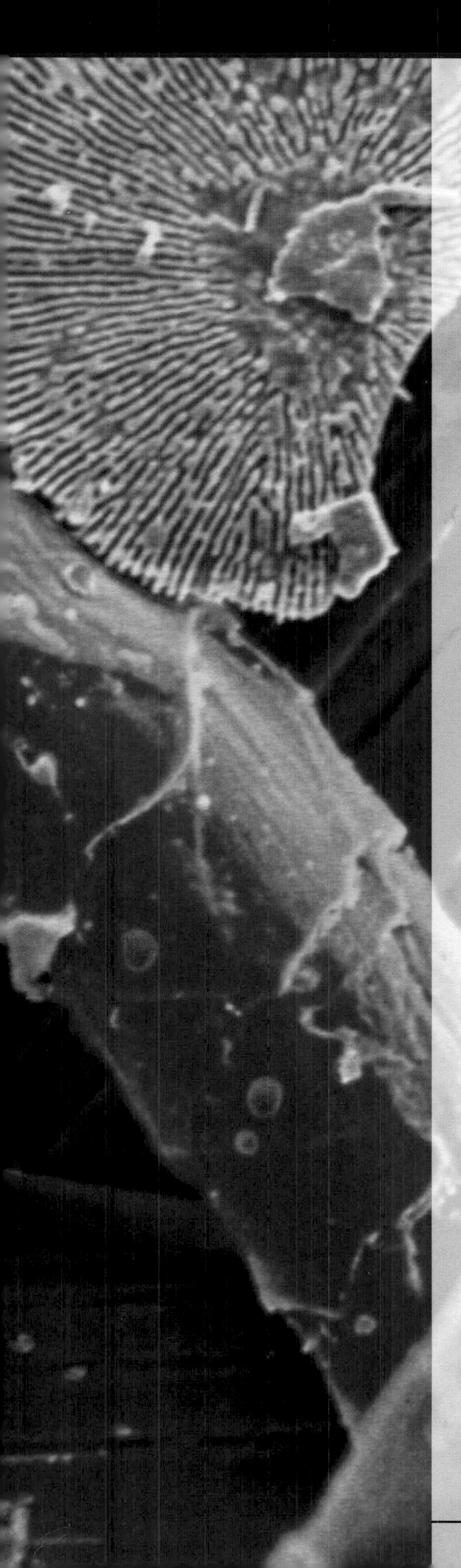

The word 'forensic' means 'connected with the courtroom'. It describes any kind of expert testimony that will be given in court at a criminal trial. The evidence of a crime can be of two kinds. Firstly, there is the event itself, and the descriptions given by witnesses, police investigators, and others associated with the event. Secondly, there is physical evidence of what has been done at the scene of the crime. Forensic scientists analyse this evidence and work out how it is connected to the crime.

MANY CRIMES

There are many different sorts of crime: burglary and theft; fraud and extortion; arson and explosion; kidnapping and abduction; vicious assault, and — most horrible of all — murder. All of these are likely to require analysis of the evidence by forensic scientists. Without the help of forensic science, it is likely that thousands of crimes would remain unsolved, or even undetected. It is only in the last 200 years that scientific examination of crime has gradually developed, but now there are specialists in every field of investigation. If there is a victim of violence or murder, his or her body — dead or alive — will be examined by a medical expert, known as a **pathologist**. What this examiner discovers will then be further investigated by one or more experts in other scientific subjects.

Forensic scientists look to human tissue and bone to provide clues that might help solve a crime.

When police are called to the scene of a serious crime, the area is immediately cordoned off in order to prevent contamination of vital evidence.

EXPERT AREAS

Some forensic scientists specialize in detecting and identifying fingerprints, while other experts called **serologists** investigate blood and other body fluids found at a crime scene. **Ballistics** experts study guns and bullets, while **biologists** identify seeds and other plant and animal **traces**, and can tell how long a dead body has lain undiscovered, by the different species of insect that have fed upon it. Other scientists keep records of paint and glass **samples**, hairs and fibres, different makes of tyres and other manufactured products. If a pathologist's report suggests the victim has been poisoned, **toxicologists** are called in to find out how. If there is no body, but just bones remaining, **anthropologists** can tell the age, sex, height, and even the race, of a skeleton's bones. Handwriting experts can show who was responsible for a written message, while psychologists can look at the scene of a crime, and describe the sort of person who may have committed it.

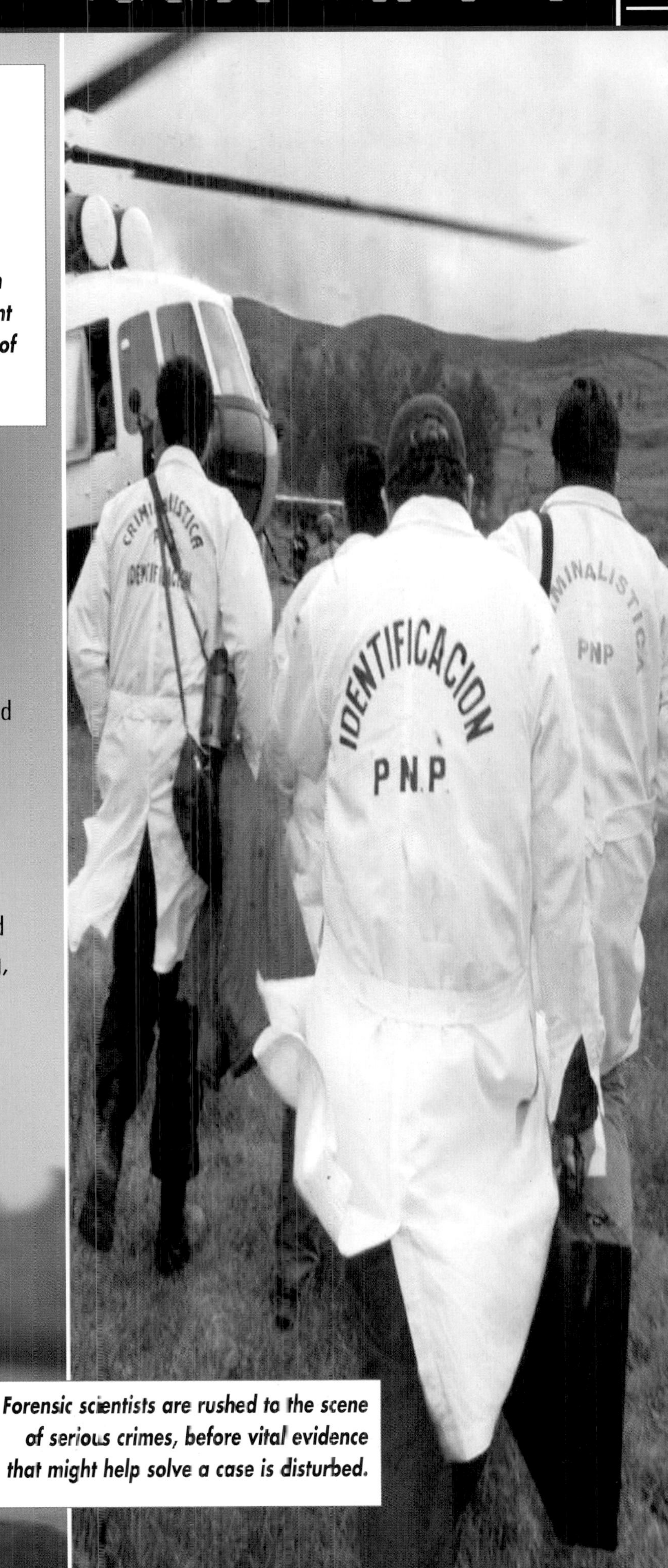

Forensic scientists are rushed to the scene of serious crimes, before vital evidence that might help solve a case is disturbed.

About 100 years ago, a French scientist called Dr Edmond Locard defined the first rule of crime investigation. It was: 'Every contact leaves a trace'. What this means is that any criminal will – often without realising – leave something behind at the scene of the crime and take something away with them.

THE SCENE OF THE CRIME

The person who has the job of examining a crime scene is called the Scene of Crime Officer (**SOCO**). Even before he or she arrives, other officers close off the scene with tapes so that nobody can disturb the evidence. The SOCO is responsible for making sure that every tiny piece of **trace** evidence is found, and saved. There will usually be a team to help in the search. It is important that they do not themselves bring traces from outside to the scene. To prevent such contamination, every member of the crime team must wear disposable paper overalls, with clean plastic overshoes and gloves.

COLLECTING EVIDENCE

Once a crime scene has been cordened off, a search team slowly and carefully searches every inch of the site for something that should not normally be there. Every little piece of evidence that is found is put into a separate bag or box, with a note of exactly where it was collected. The container is sealed, and initialled by one or more officers.

SCIENCE CONCEPTS

THE CHAIN OF CUSTODY

Trace evidence that has been found and identified may be needed in the courtroom at trial. It is very important that a record is kept of everyone who handles it. If there is any doubt, it cannot be considered at the trial. This is what happened at the trial of American football star O.J. Simpson, when the ***defence*** *suggested that blood* ***samples*** *may have been interfered with.*

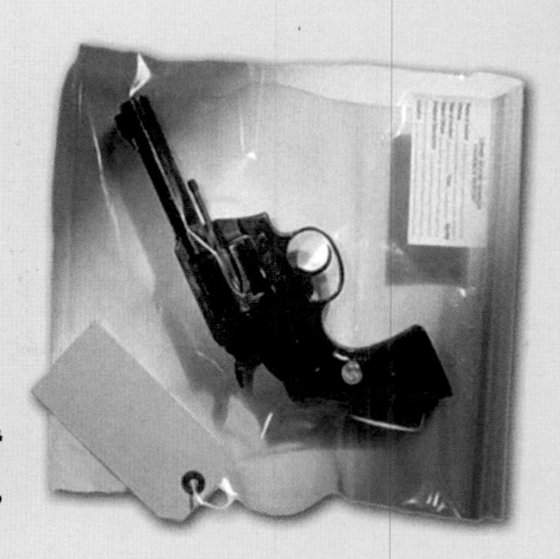

Evidence found at the crime scene must immediately be bagged to prevent contamination.

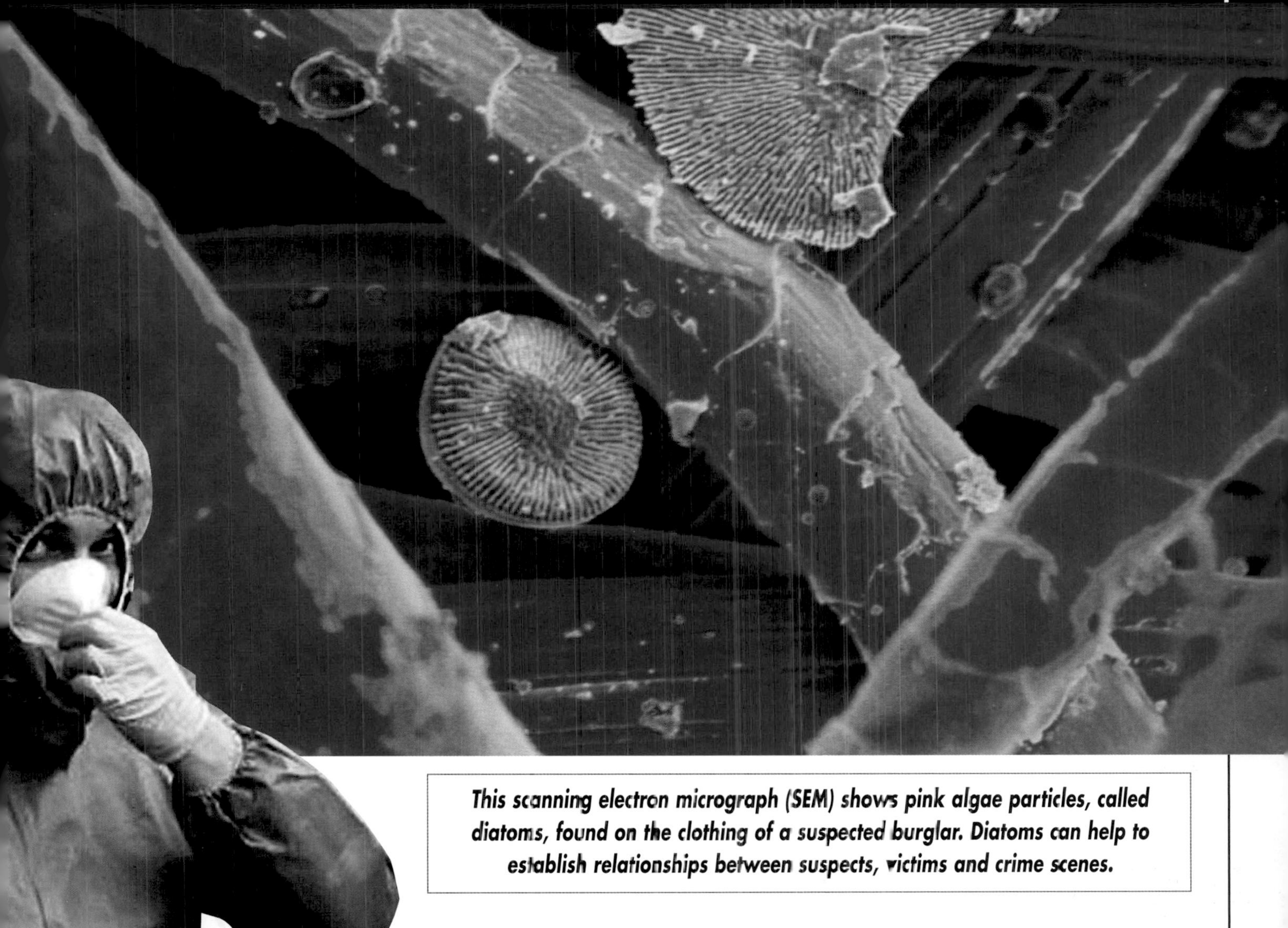

This scanning electron micrograph (SEM) shows pink algae particles, called diatoms, found on the clothing of a suspected burglar. Diatoms can help to establish relationships between suspects, victims and crime scenes.

It goes to the evidence room at the police station, then to a **forensic** expert for examination and analysis. Evidence found at the scene of a crime might include a fingerprint, a hair, some fibres from a sweater, or a footprint. It could be a used bullet, a cigarette end, or a written note. What the criminal takes away could be spots of blood from someone they have attacked, or a scratch on the face. It could be mud or sand from the scene, embedded in the sole of a shoe or a car tyre. It could be something stolen, or fragments of the victim's clothing. This trace, however tiny, could turn out to be the most important piece of evidence in solving a crime.

Scene of Crime Officers wear disposable clothing to avoid contaminating vital evidence recovered from the scene.

SCIENCE SNAPSHOT

Even the tiniest speck of dust might be the clue that helps to solve a crime. When the SOCO has to search indoors, he or she can use a small vacuum cleaner held in the hand. This can suck up trace evidence from cracks in the floorboards, and around the edges of a room.

The patterns of raised lines on the ends of our fingers are formed before we are born, and stay with us throughout our lives.

Fingerprints are one of the most important pieces of evidence in a crime. They can prove that a suspect was present at the scene, and they can also help to identify an unknown dead person. This is because no two people – not even identical twins – have the same fingerprints.

WE ARE ALL UNIQUE

The pattern of lines on our fingertips, palms and on the soles of the feet begin to form about five months before we are born, and remain the same throughout our whole lives. One of the first to discover this was a Scottish doctor, Henry Faulds, working in a Japanese hospital 130 years ago. He and his students tried all sorts of ways to make their fingertips smooth, but every time the same pattern grew back. About the same time, an English magistrate in India called William Herschel, working on a case of fraud, noticed that fingerprints could be used to

SCIENCE CONCEPTS

a) Radial Loop

b) Ulnar Loop

c) Plain Arch

d) Tented Arch

e) Plain Whorl

f) Central Pocket Whorl

g) Double Loop

h) Accidental

CLASSIFYING FINGERPRINTS

The basic method of sorting fingerprints was introduced by British policeman Sir Edward Henry in 1901. Here are eight typical patterns – two types of plain loop (a and b); a plain arch (c); tented arch (d); plain whorl (e); central pocket whorl (f); double loop (g); and 'accidental' (h).

Car tyres leave patterns a little like fingerprints in the road. These marks are all individual to a particular make and model of tyre.

distinguish one person from another, and so helped to prevent fraud. However, it took 30 more years to work out a way of describing individual prints. London's Scotland Yard led the way in 1901, and now every police force in the world has special departments for fingerprint analysis.

Fingerprints can be revealed by dusting a surface with fine powders. Here, prints on a polystyrene tile have been revealed with fine iron particles, the excess being removed from the surrounding areas using a magnet.

MANY METHODS

Prints are left by minute **traces** of sweat. If a fine powder is blown or brushed across them, it will stick and show them up. This is still the standard method of searching for prints, but in recent years other techniques have been discovered, some almost by accident. One method uses the fumes from super-glue to show up prints. Another reveals prints by laser light. Various chemical sprays can also be used.

COLLECTING FINGERPRINTS

When a suspect in a crime is detained, his or her prints will be taken. All ten fingers and thumbs are covered with printer's ink, and pressed on to a standard card. Nowadays, computers are often used instead. Each finger is scanned, and registered directly on to a computer database. This can be very rapidly compared with prints previously taken.

SCIENCE SNAPSHOT

When forensic scientists are called to outdoor crime scenes, one of the items they look for are car tyre marks. These can prove as important as fingerprints. Casts and photographs are taken. Forensic laboratories keep records of the many different patterns of tyre treads. These will identify the maker of the tyres, and often the model of car to which they were fitted.

In most cases, death is not a shock. People usually die of old age, or as the result of a serious illness. But if their death is sudden, there is always a suspicion of murder or suicide. If there is any doubt about the cause of death, the body must be examined by an expert called a pathologist at an autopsy.

EXAMINATION BY AUTOPSY

'Autopsy' means 'seeing for oneself'. It is also called 'post mortem', a Latin term that means 'after death'. In some cases the cause of death might initially appear obvious, but the pathologist still has to investigate to make sure. For example, a dead person might appear to have committed suicide by hanging. If a pathologist did not examine the body closely, they might miss the knife wound in the back of the neck that changes this from a case of suicide into one of murder.

CLUES FROM THE BODY

During an autopsy, the body is laid out on an autopsy table, cut open, and every part examined for injury. The pathologist makes a cut behind the ear down to the groin to open up the body. Any wounds are carefully examined, and items such as bullets removed from the body. The internal organs – the stomach and intestines, the heart and lungs – are all taken out and sent for analysis.

SCIENCE CONCEPTS

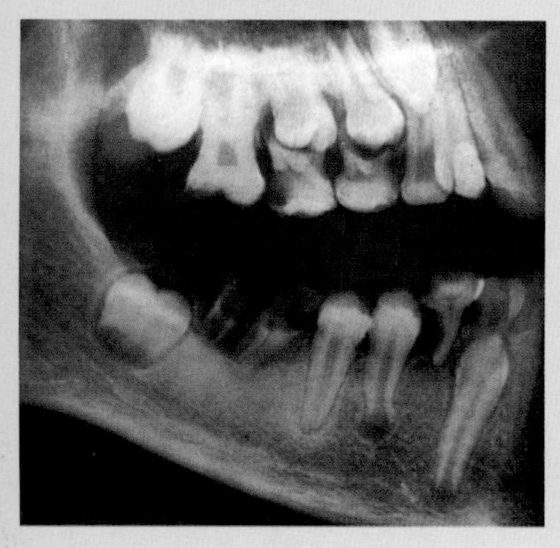

DENTAL RECORDS

Teeth can be very important in identification. Most people pay regular visits to the dentist, who keeps a detailed record, often including x-rays. In cases of severe fire, the teeth may be the only means of identification. The expert who matches dental records to the teeth of an unidentified person is called an **odontologist**.

This is a facial reconstruction of a victim of the Kings Cross fire disaster in London, England, in 1987. Experts built up a likeness from a skull discovered down an escalator shaft.

This is particularly important if poisoning is suspected. The brain is removed for later examination, and the inside of the skull checked for old injuries. An experienced pathologist can complete an autopsy in under an hour.

IDENTIFICATION

In many cases of murder it is difficult to identify the victim, especially if the body has been reduced to a skeleton. **Forensic anthropologists** use the shape of the skull and pelvis to tell whether the victim was male or female. Age can be estimated from how the bones of the skull have joined together over the years, or the condition of the bones in the arms and legs. With only a single arm or leg bone, an anthropologist can also guess at the height of the person as the length of these bones is directly related to a person's height.

Before a body is placed on an autopsy table it is weighed, measured and all distinguishing features recorded.

SCIENCE SNAPSHOT

In some cases, it is not possible to immediately identify a body because of the condition in which it is found. Sometimes, only a skeleton is found by police. Experts can now reconstruct the face from the skull. Using their knowledge, they build up the muscles and skin with modelling clay. Glass eyes are inserted, hair is added to the head, and then it is painted to look lifelike. Many unidentified bodies have been recognized by relatives or acquaintances in this way.

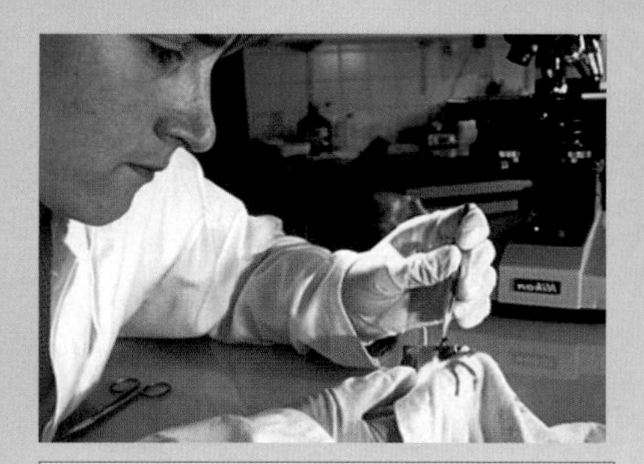

A forensic scientist extracts a **sample** of blood from a stained cloth for analysis.

Forensic serology is the study of blood and other bodily fluids for identification purposes following a crime. Forensic serologists are also in the forefront of the modern techniques of DNA profiling, which offer the possibility of positive identification of an individual by any available body cells.

BRILLIANT BLOOD

Blood is often found at the scene of a violent crime. This may not only be the victim's blood, but also that of their attacker, if there has been a struggle. By studying blood splatter patterns, scientists can begin to work out how an attack happened. In the 1930s, the Scottish **pathologist** John Glauster grouped blood splashes into six distinctive types. Blood that drops vertically will form round spots, and if it falls from a height there will be a 'crown' of tiny droplets round the edges. If the victim is struck more than once, there will be a spray of blood from the weapon. This will form streaked spots on any nearby surface, shaped rather like an exclamation mark. If one of the victim's arteries is severed, the pumping action of the heart will send great spurts of blood over a distance, and can indicate the direction in which the fatal blow was struck. Other **traces** of blood can show whether the victim's body has been moved.

OTHER FLUIDS

At a crime scene, other body fluids will often be found. Sweat can be found, together with mucus, on a discarded paper tissue, for example. Saliva can be detected on a cigarette end, or in a bite mark on the victim. In cases of sexual attack, there will usually be semen. Scientists can also sometimes tell a person's **blood group** from their saliva, semen, urine, sweat and other tissue fluids. This is because 80 percent of people are '**secretors**' – this means that their blood group can be determined from the fluids that they secrete.

DNA ANALYSIS

DNA is an extremely long **molecule**, shaped like a tightly twisted ladder. No people apart from identical

SCIENCE CONCEPTS

BLOOD GROUPS

The four basic types of blood are called A, B, AB, and O (shown left). The average proportions of the different types in a population are: A, 42 percent; B, 8 percent; O, 47 percent, and AB, 3 percent. Determining a suspect's blood type can often quickly eliminate someone from police enquiries. It is also possible to determine if blood found at a crime scene belongs to a man or a woman. Female blood cells have a centre called a Barr body, which shows up when tested in a laboratory. Men do not have the Barr body in their cells.

twins have the same DNA, and all the cells of the body – except the red blood cells – contain this substance. Analysis of short fragments of the DNA 'ladder' makes it possible to identify any individual. When DNA from a crime scene can be shown to be the same as that of a suspect, the criminal has been positively identified. The inventor of what is called 'DNA fingerprinting' was the English scientist Professor Alec Jeffreys. The detailed analysis takes a long time, but quicker methods have been developed in the United States. They make use of special **enzymes** to multiply a few molecules of DNA into many thousands. This is called the 'polymerase chain reaction', or PCR.

A forensic scientist examines a DNA printout.

A scientist removes a speck of blood from a murder weapon.

SCIENCE SNAPSHOT

Sometimes, the wrong people are sent to prison for a crime they did not commit. In Britain, a teenager who had confessed to a murder in 1986 was released when DNA analysis proved that his DNA did not match that from the crime. In the United States, lawyer Barry Scheck has set up the Innocence Project, to test the DNA of people who claimed to be wrongly imprisoned. By April 2002, 104 convicted people had been proved to be innocent.

TIME OF DEATH

In cases of sudden death – particularly if murder is suspected – it is essential to try to work out when the person died. This may be important for insurance claims. Or, if a relative has died at about the same time, there may be questions of who will inherit. The calculation can also confirm – or destroy – the alibi of a murder suspect.

LOOKING FOR CLUES

The only way to tell the exact time of death is to be there when it happens. However, **forensic** scientists have several methods of working out an approximate time of death. The moment a person dies, his or her body begins to cool steadily. Taking the temperature can give a rough estimate of how long it has been cooling, but only within several hours. A condition known as **rigor mortis** provides scientists with another way of estimating the time of death. Some hours after a person has died, the body muscles begin to stiffen. The face muscles begin to tighten within 1-4 hours of death, and the limbs in 4-6 hours. After 12 hours, bacteria begin to **decompose** the tissues, and the muscles relax.

CLUES FROM THE STOMACH

During an **autopsy** the **pathologist** will examine the contents of the stomach and small intestine, particularly if poisoning is suspected. There may be partially digested food there, or the organs may be empty. The exposed stomach must be slid away from the other abdominal organs and manoeuvered over a large container. The wall of the stomach is opened with scissors and the contents collected.

(right) Measuring body temperature helps scientists to work out the approximate time of death.

The person must still have been alive when they last ate. So, if the time of their last meal can be discovered, this is another rough indication of when they died.

Entomologists also look at the type of insects found on a corpse to work out when a person died. This red-legged ham beetle arrives some time after death and feeds on a body's dried fats.

INSECT INVADERS

From the moment of death, insects begin to arrive at the body. First to come are the blowflies. They lay their eggs, and in a few hours these hatch out into maggots, which begin feeding on the flesh. During the next ten to twelve days, the maggots grow and shed their skins twice, before leaving to form pupae, and then emerge as adult flies. Entomologists – insect **biologists** – can therefore tell how many days have passed since the eggs were laid. Over days, weeks and months, other insects arrive in a known order. All these can help to indicate how long ago death took place.

(right) Blowfly lavae can appear on corpses just a few hours after death.

SCIENCE CONCEPTS

LIFE CYCLES

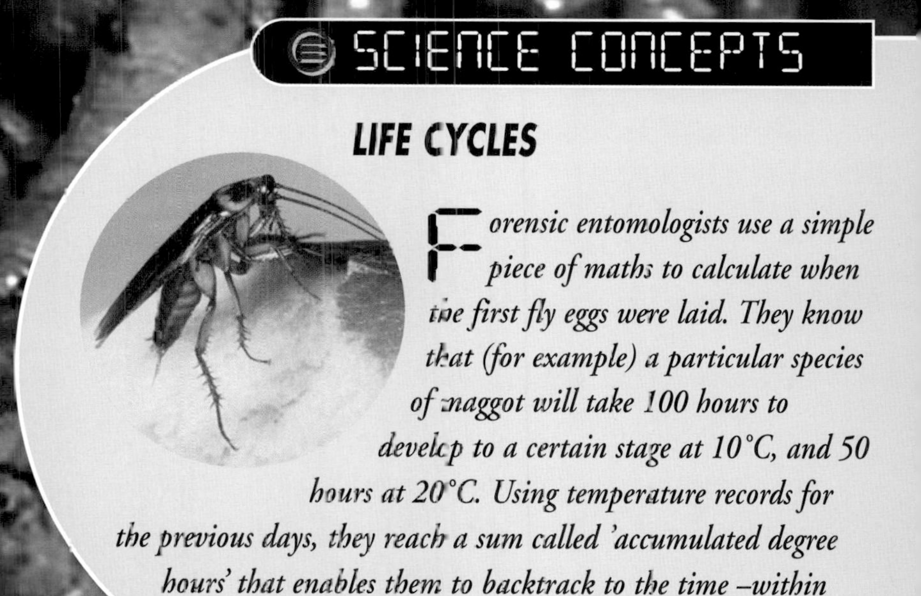

Forensic entomologists use a simple piece of maths to calculate when the first fly eggs were laid. They know that (for example) a particular species of maggot will take 100 hours to develop to a certain stage at 10°C, and 50 hours at 20°C. Using temperature records for the previous days, they reach a sum called 'accumulated degree hours' that enables them to backtrack to the time –within an hour or two –when the maggots first emerged.

SCIENCE SNAPSHOT

MYSTERIOUS LIQUIDS

As bacteria gradually decompose a dead body, liquids begin to seep out into the surroundings. An American scientist named Arpad Vass made a chemical analysis of the different compounds in the liquids, and the times at which they appeared. Now, he and his colleagues have developed an electronic 'nose', which can detect these compounds, and so calculate how long the body has been lying where it was found.

THE SMOKING GUN

In modern times, more and more murders are committed with guns. The murderer usually takes his gun away from the scene, but trace evidence remains. Often the shells from the fired bullets can be found scattered around the scene, while the bullets themselves will be embedded in the victim. The science of firearm examination is known as 'ballistics'.

LOOKING FOR THE GROOVE

Almost all firearms are rifled. This means that the inside of the barrel is cut into spiral grooves, to spin the bullet and make the aim more accurate. These grooves cause marks called striations along the length of the bullet. Every gun manufacturer cuts the grooves in a slightly different way, so it is easy to determine the make and model of gun by examining the bullet.

SCIENCE CONCEPTS

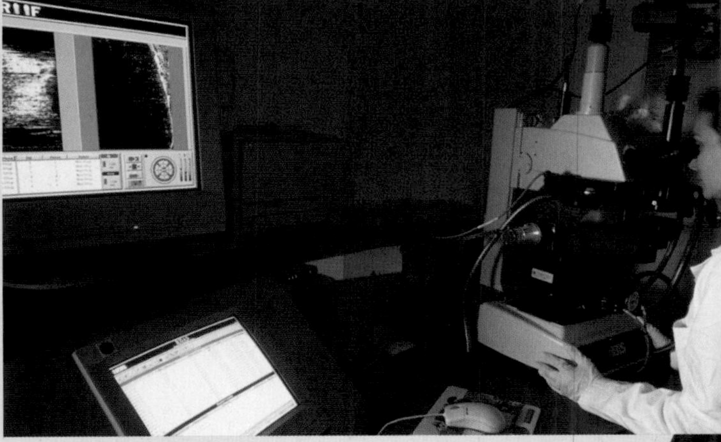

COMPARING BULLETS

The science of ballistics was established in 1920 by an American called Charles Waite. He spent two years collecting data from gun manufacturers all over the United States and Europe. One of his colleagues invented a special microscope – the comparison microscope – in which two bullets could be laid side-by-side, and the markings on them compared directly.

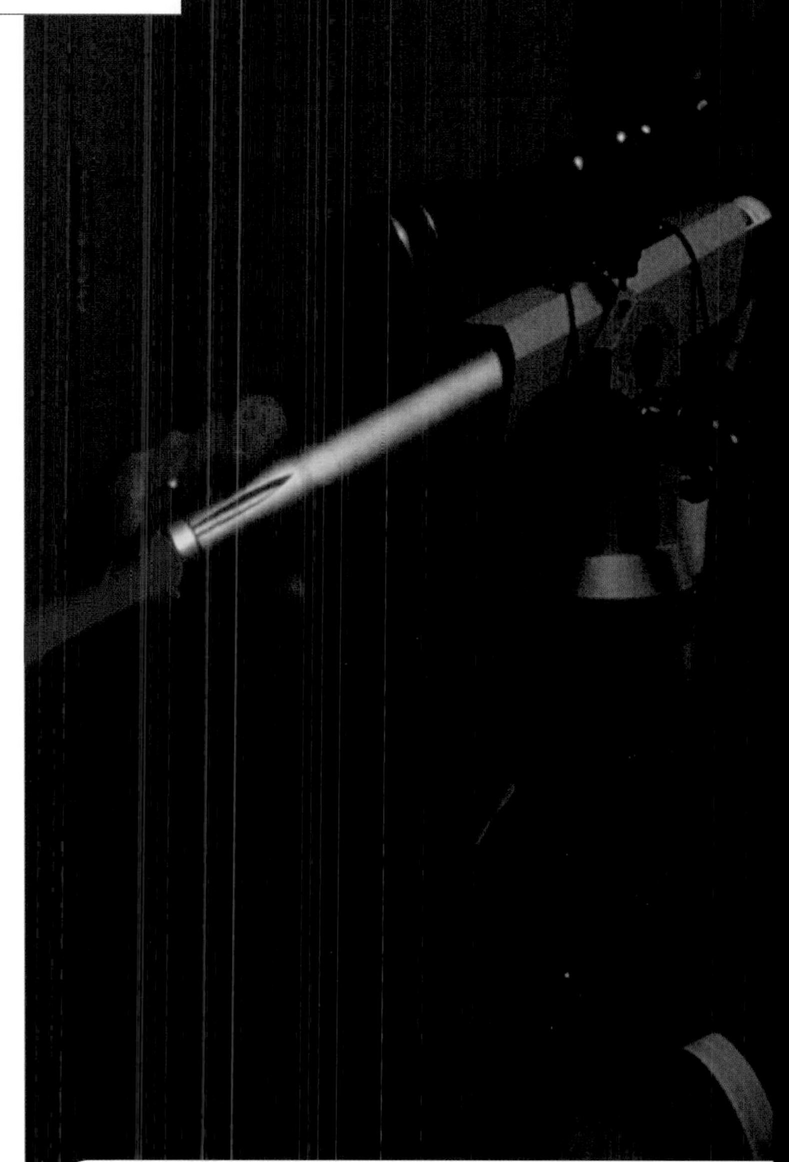

Laser sights are used to determine the path of a bullet.

SHELL SECRETS

Shells – empty bullet cases – recovered from the scene also provide important clues about the type of firearm used in the crime. A shell lies against a steel 'breech-block' and is fired by a 'firing pin'. As the gun is fired, the pin leaves a mark on the base of the shell. The force of the firing also drives the shell back against the breech-block, and this leaves an impression of any manufacturing imperfections, or wear. These can help to identify the individual gun used. If police recover a weapon they suspect was used to commit a crime, to provide **forensic** evidence, test bullets are fired from this gun, and the markings compared with those from the scene of the crime.

CLUES FROM THE POWDER

All guns rely on explosives to fire bullets. When a gun is fired, tiny particles of the remains of the explosive powder are blown back, and can settle on the hands or clothing of the firer. Whenever a suspect suspected of a gun crime is arrested, their hands are examined by forensic investigators. Swabs are taken and sent to the laboratory for testing. Scientists analyse for minute traces of **nitrates** from the explosive, or use an electron microscope to detect particles of **barium** or **antimony**, all strengthening the case against a suspect.

When forensic scientists handle evidence, they always wear protective clothing to prevent contamination of the evidence.

SCIENCE SNAPSHOT

The path of a bullet through a human body can change dramatically. The most famous example of this is the assassination of President Kennedy One of the two bullets that killed him passed through his head and throat before striking Governer Connally and passing through his back and chest, dropping out on the floor of the car. Today, firearms experts use a laser-beam sight, aligned through the marks found on a victim or crime scene, to discover the direction the bullet was fired from, and from approximately how far away.

Criminals can sometimes be trapped by the words they use, and the way they use them. Kidnappers send notes demanding ransom, while others write letters to newspapers, or make taunting telephone calls to the police, or the relatives of their victims. Forgers produce written or printed documents that are fakes. Unfortunately for the criminal, these letters reveal important clues which help the police to catch them.

SECRETS FROM THE SCRIPT

It is almost impossible to disguise your handwriting entirely. **Graphologists** can detect a person's characteristics through their handwriting. In court, these experts give evidence comparing two pieces of writing, testifying that they were written by the same person. This is particularly valuable in cases of kidnapping or forgery. In 1935, Bruno Hauptmann was convicted of the kidnapping and death of Charles Lindbergh's baby son, partially on the evidence of the similarity of his handwriting and that on the ransom note.

WORD WISE

The words that a criminal uses – whether in speech or text – can also help in identification. One non-criminal case is particularly famous. The novel *Primary Colors*, a book that thinly disguised the actions of American president Bill Clinton, was published in 1996 by an author known simply as 'Anonymous'.

SCIENCE CONCEPTS

THE UNABOMBER

For 17 years, the FBI hunted for a man who built booby-trap bombs, and often sent them through the post. He was responsible for three deaths and 29 serious injuries, and was known as the 'Unabomber'. In 1995, he sent a 35,000-word 'manifesto' to two American newspapers. An American professor read this, and recognized the style of her brother-in-law, Ted Kaczynski. When the FBI raided Kaczynski's lonely cabin in the mountains, they found his bomb-making equipment there. Kaczynski was sentenced to life imprisonment in 1996.

Scientists work using a computerized handwriting recognition system.

An American professor analysed the text on his computer, and found many unusual words and phrases that identified the author as a well-known journalist. After this success, the professor was consulted by the Federal Bureau of Investigation (FBI) in a number of criminal cases. Psychologists, also, can tell a great deal about the personality of a person from the words and phrases that they use.

VOICE DETECTIVES

Sometimes a criminal's voice can be recorded on tape. He or she may make telephone calls to a newspaper, a radio station, or the investigating police. There are even cases in which the criminal was interviewed on television, with his back to the camera. When a suspect is arrested, a recording of the police interview can be compared by means of a 'voiceprint'. This technique, which was developed in America, makes use of an electronic analysis of the sound waves of the voice. This is valuable evidence because no two people's voiceprints are the same. Even professional mimics produce a voiceprint different from that of the person they are imitating. Experts can also detect a person's age, sex and race from the sound of his or her voice. Voiceprints have also been used to reveal slight trembling in a person's voice – a sign that they may be lying.

The novel Primary Colors was written anonymously by a journalist, who was eventually identified by the style of his writing. John Travolta (left) starred in the film version.

SCIENCE SNAPSHOT

GRAPHOLOGY

What do graphologists look for when they examine handwriting? They divide the writing into upper, middle and lower zones, and measure the relative sizes. They look whether the writing is level, or slopes up or down. They ask whether it is bold and confident, or thin and scratchy. And they examine the size and importance of individual letters, particularly 't' and 'i'.

The actor Basil Rathbone as Sherlock Holmes, Conan Doyle's famous detective.

The most famous fictional detective is Sherlock Holmes. He could tell amazing details about the nature of an unidentified criminal from subtle instances of behaviour. His creator, Sir Arthur Conan Doyle, learnt the secret from Dr Joseph Bell, who was his teacher in medicine at Edinburgh Royal Infirmary. In the last 40 years, the Federal Bureau of Investigation (FBI) in America has developed similar techniques that are known as 'psychological profiling'.

FAMILIAR METHODS

From crime to crime, criminals generally use the same methods, and behave in the same kind of way. This is known as their '**modus operandi**' (MO), which is Latin for 'way of working'. Some will deliberately leave a sign at the scene of the crime – their 'signature'. Around 1969, the FBI began to study cases of **serial killers** (those who kept on murdering innocent people). Talking to those who had been caught and sent to prison, they began to build up ideas of how their minds worked, and the ways in which they behaved. Quite soon, they were able to describe the type of person – so far unidentified – who had committed a violent crime, and predict what he or she was likely to do next. With growing experience, they were even able to describe people who had committed other crimes, such as arson (deliberately setting fire) or insurance fraud.

GLOBAL POLICE FORCE

In 1985, the FBI began to record the details of all violent crimes on computer. In this way, they were able to compare murders committed over a wide area, and decide whether the same killer was responsible. Nowadays, they train police officers from all over the world in the skills of **psychological profiling**. This method has led to the capture of many criminals including the 'Railway Rapist', John Duffy, and killer Richard Trenton Chase.

The 'railway rapist' John Duffy, captured through the use of pyschological profiling.

SCIENCE CONCEPTS

CRIME CLASSIFICATION

In 1992, the FBI published their Crime Classification Manual. Based on the records they have gathered, it listed the details of 33 different types of murder, 35 types of arson, and 46 types of sexual assault. In particular, they distinguished two general kinds of serial killers. 'Organised' killers choose their victims, and often hide the body and clean up the crime scene. 'Disorganised' killers pick their victims at random, and leave the bodies where they can soon be discovered.

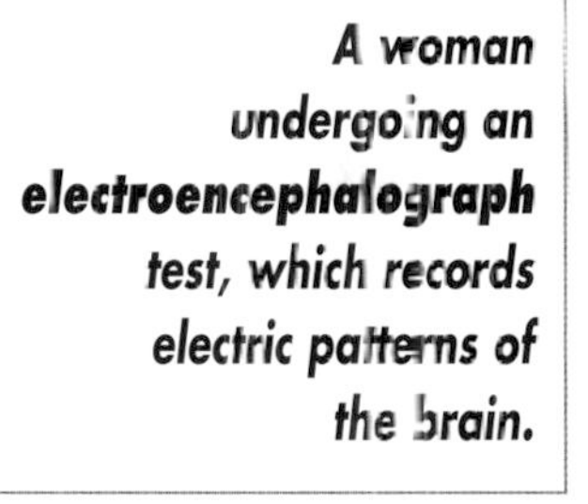

A woman undergoing an **electroencephalograph** test, which records electric patterns of the brain.

TELLING THE TRUTH?

During the 1930s, it was hoped that the polygraph (or 'lie detector') would show when a suspect lied during questioning. However, there were so many failures that it is now rarely used. The modern equivalent is the **electroencephelograph** (ECG). This scans the electrical waves that pass through the brain. It detects changes in the brain waves when a guilty person hears particular phrases, or is shown evidence from a crime, and has been given the name 'brain fingerprinting'. In America, a man who is on Death Row in Oklahoma has asked to be given this test to prove he is innocent of the murders for which he was sentenced to death.

SCIENCE SNAPSHOT

When several crimes are committed in an area, computers can draw a map that pinpoints the probable 'base of operation' of the criminal – a home district, or a social meeting-place. This technique, which has been best developed by the Canadian Mounted Police, is known as 'geographical profiling'.

Forensic laboratories keep extensive records, together with a wide range of **samples**, of most manufactured products. These include all kinds of paint and glass, paper and synthetic fibres, as well as details of clothing. When a plane exploded above the tiny Scottish town of Lockerbie in 1988, forensic investigators were able to draw on this database to track down the culprits.

"THE GADDAFI CHARITABLE ORGANISATIONS HAVE BEEN DEALING WITH THE FAMILIES TO REACH AN AGREEMENT, AND THEY HAVE REACHED AN AGREEMENT."

COLONEL GADDAFI, 1ST SEPTEMBER, 2003

DISASTER FROM THE SKY

When the PanAm 747 Maid of the Seas exploded over Lockerbie in Scotland on 21 December 1988, all 259 persons aboard perished. Huge pieces of the aircraft fell on the town, killing another 11 people, and destroying a number of houses. Smaller pieces were scattered over an area of 845 square miles (2,190 square kilometres). Some were carried 45 miles away by a strong westerly wind. Searchers eventually recovered about 4 million fragments, which were laid out at the Army Central Ammunition Depot near Lockerbie for examination. They found the pieces of a luggage container, and fragments of a brown suitcase that had been inside it. This was what had held the bomb. An accident inspector also found a tiny piece of printed circuit board. It was identified as part of a Toshiba radio-cassette player.

The Libyan leader Colonel Gaddafi, who agreed to compensate famlies of the victims.

PIECING TOGETHER THE CLUES

Researchers at the Royal Armament Research & Development Establishment (RARDE), in Fort Halsted, Kent, found more fragments of the Toshiba player, and calculated that it had been packed with about 14 ounces (400 gm) of **Semtex** explosive. Later, they found a fragment of an electronic timer that had been used to produce the explosion. Only 20 of this particular timer had been manufactured, in Switzerland, and sold to the Libyan government. More searches of the wreckage turned up some fragments of clothing, including a label 'Malta Trading Company'.

LIBYA TO BLAME?

Police inquiries in Malta led to the discovery of the trader who had sold the clothing —and he was able to describe the Libyan man who had bought it. Three years later, the American and Scottish authorities named two Libyan men as responsible for the bomb. In 1999, the two men were finally brought to trial, at a special court set up in the Netherlands. In January 2001 only one was found guilty —but doubts are still expressed about the verdict. Nevertheless, in August 2003, the Libyan leader, Colonel Gaddafi, announced that 2.7 billion dollars would be paid as compensation to the relatives of the victims of the Lockerbie bombing.

- *PanAm Flight 903 was destroyed in the air by an explosion on 21 December 1988.*
- *The explosion was caused by a bomb in a suitcase in the luggage compartment.*
- *Some 4 million pieces of the aircraft were gathered and examined.*
- *The bomb was a radio-cassette player packed with Semtex. It had been triggered by an unusual make of electronic timer.*
- *The timer had been purchased by the Libyan government.*
- *Fragments of clothing led to the identification of two Libyan men.*

Commemorative tombstones show the names of those who perished during the Lockerbie disaster.

Even when a body has completely decomposed, the bones left behind still provide a wealth of forensic evidence. Anthropologists are able to identify the age and sex of the person, and calculate his or her height. Faced with a jumble of bones from several different people, they can sort them out. The latest analytical methods also make it possible to extract DNA from the bones. All of these methods were used to help solve the riddle of the Romanovs.

DEATH OF THE ROYALS

Following the Russian Revolution of 1917, Tsar Nicholas II, his wife, and five children —the Romanov royal family — were imprisoned in a house in Siberia. On the night of 16 July 1918 they, together with their doctor and servants, were executed by firing squad. Six months later, Russian investigator Nicholas Sokolov announced that the bodies had been thrown down a disused mine shaft, soaked in sulphuric acid, and finally consumed by fire.

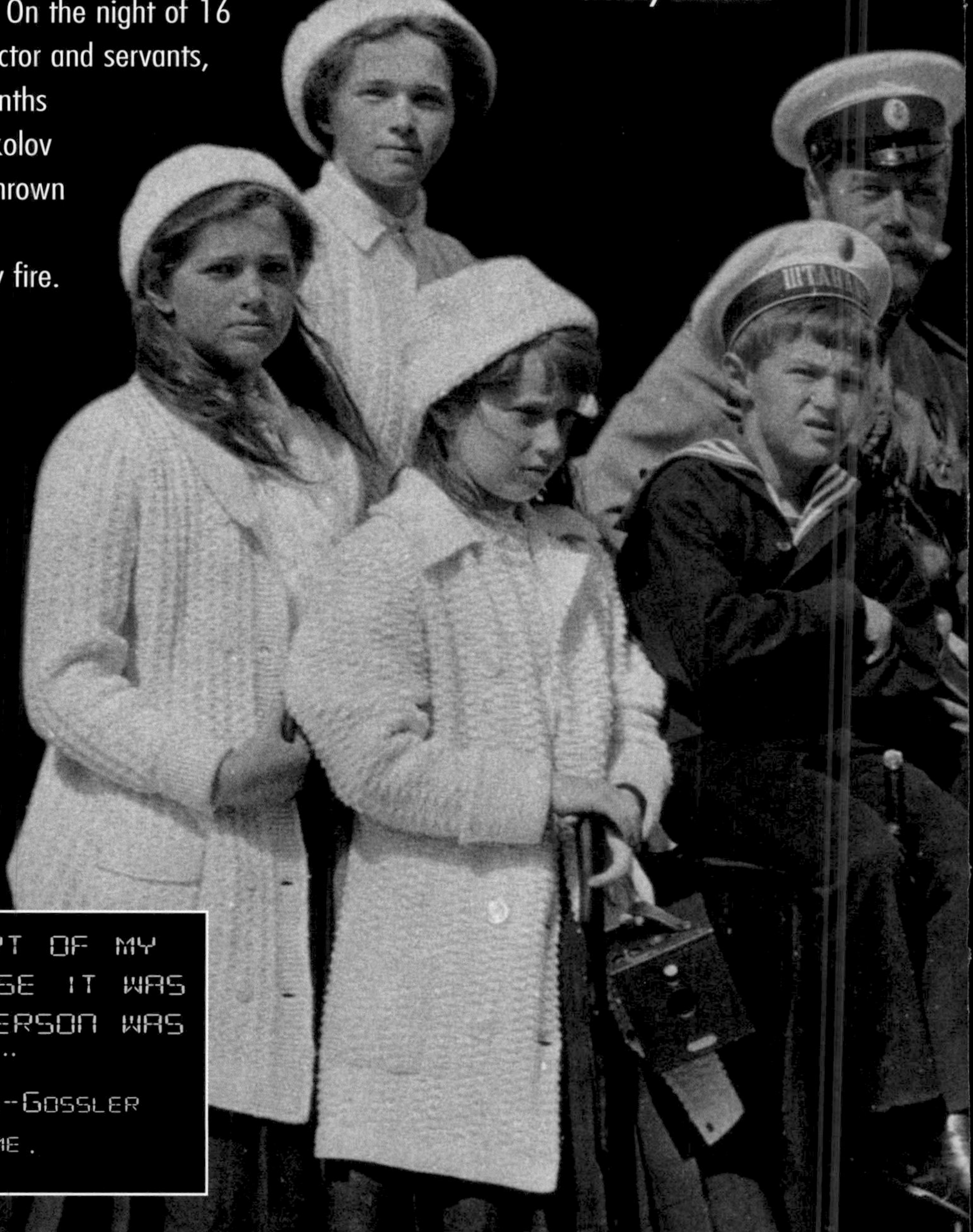

Tsar Nicholas II, picture with his family, shortly before they were brutally executed.

NEW CLUES

However, in 1989, a film-maker named Gely Ryabov announced that he had found bones and scraps of clothing at a site five miles (eight kilometres) away from the mine-shaft. In 1991, Soviet president Boris Yeltsin gave permission for the site to be excavated. Around 1,000 pieces of bone and skulls were unearthed, and assembled into four male and five

"FROM THE VERY START OF MY INVOLVEMENT IN THE CASE IT WAS CLEAR TO ME ANNA ANDERSON WAS SCHANZKOWSKA."
SAYS DR. VON BERENBERG-GOSSLER IN HIS HAMBURG HOME.

The story of Anastasia was made into a film in 1956, starring Ingrid Bergman (right).

female skeletons. Russian scientists identified the skulls, and decided that two were missing, those of the Tsar's son Alexei, and his daughter Marie.

SOLVING THE MYSTERY?

However, a team of American experts suggested that the missing skull was that of another daughter, Anastasia. The bones were taken to England by a Russian DNA expert, who carried out analyses with a scientist from the British Forensic Science Service. They found that five of the bodies were related, and included three females. The Tsarina was identified by means of a DNA **sample** provided by her grandnephew, the Duke of Edinburgh. To prove the identity of the Tsar, the tomb of his brother was opened, and DNA analysis proved the two men were brothers.

A NEW TWIST

Despite this success, eleven people were believed to have died in Yekaterinburg, and only nine skeletons were found. For many years, there had been rumours that Alexei and Anastasia had escaped execution. A woman named Anna Anderson had claimed all her life that she was Anastasia. An American hospital had kept a sample of her tissue after an operation, and in 1994, 10 years after her death, DNA analysis proved that she was not a Romanov. She was a Polish peasant named Franzisca Schanzkowska, and members of the Schanzkowska family provided DNA samples that confirmed this.

- *Modern methods make it possible to extract DNA from old bones.*
- *Even a mix of the bones of a number of skeletons can be separated and identified by forensic anthropologists.*
- *Most of the bodies of the Romanov family were not destroyed in a mine-shaft, but buried five miles away.*
- *Nine skeletons of the family and their servants were discovered, but two remained missing.*
- *Five of the skeletons were positively identified as those of the Tsar, his wife, and three daughters. (Anna Anderson, who claimed to be the missing Anastasia, was revealed as an impostor.*

The bones of members of the Romanov family, identified by forensic scientists.

For many hundreds of years, poisoning was a popular way of murdering somebody. However, although the effects of the poison were obvious, there was no way to discover what the poison was. It was not until the the 19th century that the science of toxicology (the study of poisons) was founded. Toxicology has solved many past murders, including the death of the explorer Charles Francis Hall.

Dr Emil Bessels, the chief scientist on board the Polaris.

EARLY POISONERS

The commonest poison used by murderers in the 19th century was arsenic. This is a white powder, with a faint sweet taste that is easily disguised by stronger-flavoured food. People poisoned with arsenic are violently ill, and doctors frequently decided that they had died from an acute gastric disease. Arsenic was widely used as a rat poison, which was sold at pharmacies or household stores —even to young children. In the 1830s, an English chemist named James Marsh worked out a test for very small quantities of arsenic in the body. The test was used successfully in a famous French case of murder, and soon afterwards many countries made laws controlling the sale of arsenic. Nevertheless, cases of murder by arsenic continued.

"I AM THE COMMANDING OFFICER OF THIS VESSEL," HALL FUMED. "I ORDERED YOU TO KEEP MY JOURNAL. YOU ARE TO WRITE WHAT I DICTATE."

EXTRACT FROM THE EXPEDITION'S JOURNAL

DEATH OF A HERO

In 1871, Charles Francis Hall led an American expedition into the Arctic, in search of the North Pole. Aboard a naval steam tug, the Polaris, he reached the north coast of Greenland, about 500 miles from the Pole. He decided to spend the winter there, and named the place Thank God Harbor. From the beginning of the voyage, Hall had quarreled with his chief scientist, a German named Dr Emil Bessels. One evening Hall drank a cup of coffee, and was very soon violently sick.

Today, scientists find it easy to detect the presence of poisons such as arsenic.

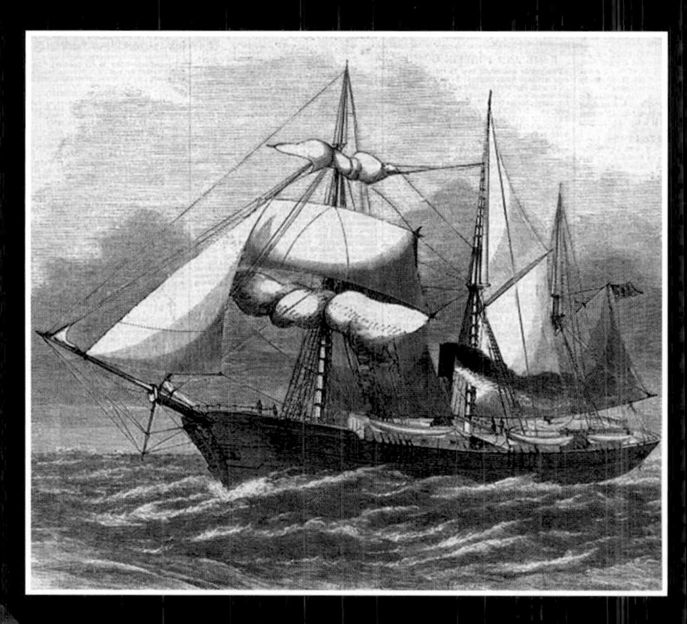

A 19th century illustration of Hall's ship, the Polaris.

He took to his bed, where Dr Bessels treated him. Hall gradually grew worse, and two weeks later he died and was buried on shore. His crew suspected that he had been poisoned, but the truth was not known for nearly a century.

THE MYSTERY SOLVED

In 1968, two scientists flew to Thank God Harbor, and dug up Hall's body. They took **samples** of hair and a fingernail, and these were analysed at the Toronto Center of **Forensic** Sciences in Canada. Scientists used a modern technique called **neutron activation analysis**. Enough arsenic was found in Hall's fingernail to indicate that he had received a huge dose during the last two weeks of his life.

CASE STUDY FACTFILE

- *Charles Hall, Arctic explorer, died on the north coast of Greenland in 1871.*
- *Analysis performed in 1968 showed that Hall had almost certainly been poisoned with arsenic.*
- *The expedition's chief scientist, Dr Emil Bessels, has always been the principal suspect.*
- *When a person is poisoned with arsenic, the poison can be found in their fingernails and hair.*
- *Until the mid-19th century, arsenic was freely on sale.*
- *The first accurate analytical test for arsenic is known as the Marsh test, after the chemist who developed it.*
- *The chemical name of 'arsenic' is arsenious oxide.*

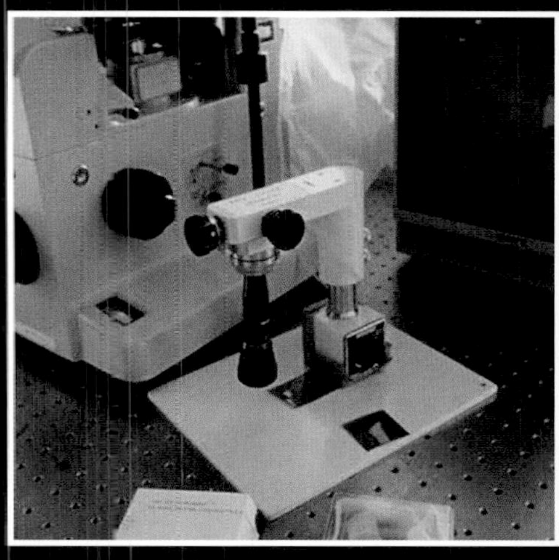

Neutron activation analysis revealed arsenic in Hall's blood.

Proving that something is a forgery can be very difficult. Chemical analysis of the ink or the paint, the paper or the canvas, means that a tiny part must be destroyed. Even carbon-dating needs a small sample. But often it is the eye of the expert alone that detects the telltale clue. These tehniques led to the eventual capture of the Mormon bomber Mark Hofmann.

PROFESSIONAL FORGER

Mark Hofmann lived in Salt Lake City, Utah. He made a profitable living forging rare documents, and selling them to the Mormon Church. In 1985, he offered a single sheet of paper to the Library of Congress, at a price of one million dollars. This was 'The Oath of a Freeman', printed in 1639, and no example was known to have survived. Photocopies of another work from the same medieval printer, the Bay Psalm Book, were easily available, and Hofmann used these to base his copy of the Oath on. He used a blank piece of paper from an old book, and made ink by burning the leather binding of another, so that carbon-dating would confirm its age. Then he had a printing plate made from his pasted-up text.

One of Hofmann's bombs went off in his car, injuring Hofmann himself.

"ALL ALONG, OF COURSE, UNTIL THE EVENING THAT I MADE THEM, I DIDN'T REALLY THINK THAT I WOULD END UP USING THEM. AT LEAST TO TAKE A LIFE."

MARK HOFMANN

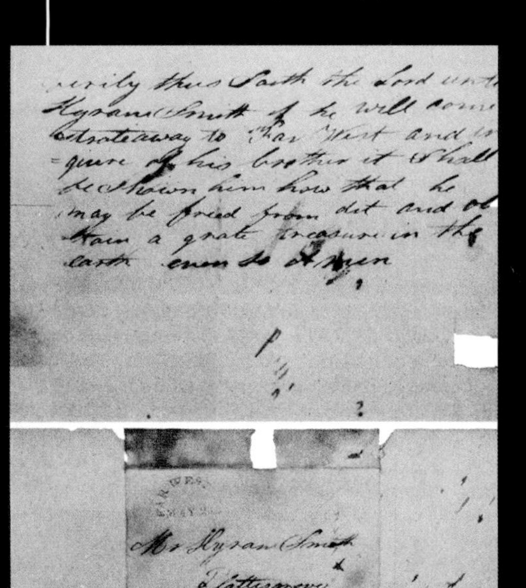
verily thus Saith the Lord unto
Hyram Smith if he will come
straitaway to Far West and in
=quire of his brother it shall
be shown him how that he
may be freed from det and ob
=tain a grate treasure in the
earth even so Amen

Mr Hyram Smith

Experts could not decide whether the Oath was genuine or not. Then a document examiner at Arizona State Crime Laboratory reported that, out of 79 documents that Hofmann had sold to the Mormon Church, 21 were likely to be forgeries.

A fake letter sold to the Mormon church by Mark Hofmann.

ON TO MURDER

To draw attention away from the inquiry, Hofmann decided to send bombs to several top members of the Church. Two people were killed. Hofmann even injured himself, with a bomb he set in his own car. In the end, it was the County Attorney who spotted that the Oath was a forgery. He had spent 17 years in the printing industry, and knew all about type. He showed how Hofmann had made photographs of the Bay Psalm Book, then cut out letter by letter, and pasted them together to make the text of the Oath. And many of the letters were closer together than if they had been set in type. In 1987 Hofmann was found guilty of two murders and many forgeries.

The forger and murderer Mark Hofmann.

CASE STUDY FACTFILE

- *A fake is a copy of a genuine document or work of art. Forgery is when the faker claims that this article is genuine. If her or she offers it for sale, that is fraud.*
- *Mark Hofmann claimed to have discovered many rare Mormon documents. Many of these were later found to be forgeries.*
- *Suspicions were raised when Hofmann offered The Oath of a Freeman for sale. No copies of this work were known to have survived.*
- *Carbon-dating can establish the age of an article that is a century or more old, but a tiny sample will be destroyed.*
- *Hofmann's ignorance of the techniques of typesetting led to his downfall.*

GLOSSARY

Alibi A Latin word that means 'elsewhere'. A suspect is brought in for questioning by the police: if he or she can prove that they were not near the scene of the crime at the time it was committed, they have 'established an alibi'.

Anthropologist A scientist who studies the remains of human beings and cultures.

Antimony A poisonous metallic element.

Autopsy A word meaning 'seeing for oneself'. The detailed examination by a pathologist of a dead body to determine cause of death. Also known as 'post mortem'.

Ballistics The study of the path that a projectile – such as a bullet – takes. This word is now commonly applied to the technical examination of bullets and firearms involved in crimes.

Barium A metallic element related to potassium and sodium

Biologist A scientist concerned with the nature of all living things. Entomology, the study of the behavior of insects, is particularly important in calculating how long a body has been dead.

Blood groups All human blood is of one of four groups: A, B, AB or O.

Carbon-dating Method of finding out the age of an object by measuring the level of radiaactive carbon in it.

Cells The 'building-blocks' of living things. All except red blood cells contain a nucleus, in which the DNA is unique to each individual.

Decomposed Broken down. Very soon after death, bacteria begin to digest the internal organs of the body, and gradually spread to the exterior.

Defence The lawyer, or team of lawyers, who argue in court that the person charged with committing a crime (the defendant) is innocent.

DNA Deoxyribonucleic acid. A very long and complex molecule that is present in every cell with a nucleus. (Red blood cells do not have a nucleus, and therefore do not contain DNA.) The DNA molecule is made up of genes.

Enzyme A protein produced by a living thing that sets off chemical reactions.

Forensic A word meaning 'connected with the court'.

Electroencephalograph An apparatus that detects the electrical activity of the brain, and displays it as 'waves' on a video screen.

Graphologist Someone who studies handwriting. Experts can compare two samples, or more, and say whether they were written by the same person – even if the handwriting has been disguised.

Modus Operandi Latin for 'way of working'. The characteristic way in which a criminal carries out a crime.

Molecule A combination of atoms that makes up a specific chemical compound.

Mormonism An internationally widespread religion, founded by Joseph Smith in 1831. They have their own bible, very different from the Christian Bible.

Neutron activation analysis Method used to identify extremely small traces of elements.

Nitrates Chemical compounds that provide the oxygen necessary to set off an explosive.

Pathologist A medical doctor who specializes in performing autopsies.

Pyschological profiling Preparing a description of the probable personality and future behaviour of a criminal, from a study of the nature of their crime.

Rigor mortis The stiffening of the muscles of the body that begins soon after death. It gradually fades away, due to the activities of bacteria

Sample A small quantity of material, collected for forensic examination.

Secretor A person whose blood group can be discovered from their saliva, sweat, or other body fluids.

Semtex One of the most powerful plastic explosives in the world, manufactured in the Czech Republic.

Serial killer A person who kills three or more people, with an interval of time between each murder.

Serologist Person who studies and analyses the body fluids.

Shell The outer metallic casing of a bullet, containing the explosive powder, and closed with the detonator cap. Most modern guns eject the shell after firing.

SOCO In Britain, the scene of crime officer. Nowadays, most are specialist civilian members of the police force.

Toxicologist A scientist who carries out analysis for poisons, and understands their effect upon the human body.

Trace A tiny piece of physical evidence.

First published in Great Britain in 2004 by ticktock Media Ltd.,
Unit 2, Orchard Business Centre, North Farm Road, Tunbridge Wells, Kent, TN2 3XF
We would like to thank: Elizabeth Wiggans and Jenni Rainford for their help with this book.
ISBN 1 86007 590 8 HB ISBN 1 86007 584 3 PB
Printed in China
A CIP catalogue record for this book is available from the British Library.

Picture Credits
Alamy: 14-15c, 15 all. Corbis: 4-5c, 5t, 10-11c, 14c, 18-19c, 25t, 25br, 26-27 all. Getty Images: 8l, 22-23c, 28-29 all. Reuters: 5r, 6-7c. Rex Features: 6b, 11r, 18b, 20tl, 21-22 c, 22c, 23r, 24-25c. Science Photo Library: 2-3 & 7t, 9c, 9r, 10b, 12 all, 16-17 all. 19r, 21tr,